LAST RESORT

LAST RESORT

KATHLEEN BYRD

♡ Kathleen Byrd

Last Resort ©2024 Kathleen Byrd

All rights reserved. No part of this book may be reproduced, distributed, or transmitted in any form or by any means electronic or mechanical, without the prior written permission of the publisher, except in the case of brief quotations embodied in critical articles and reviews and certain other noncommercial uses permitted by copyright law.

Cover created by Robert Ross from an image of a modified photograph taken from the International Space Station (ISS) on February 2015; *Panorama of the Pacific Northwest.*

Printed & published by
Last Word Press
in Olympia, Washington.

ISBN: 978-1-944234-60-7
First Edition 2024
10 9 8 7 6 5 4 3 2 1

*For my lineage of
Theodoras and Lamberdinas
and for the land.*

Contents

I don't know *1*

Earthopomorphizing *2*

Doubt Probably *3*

At the River Deschutes *4*

Oh Tahoma *5*

A Heron waits *6*

Non-native *7*

Dear Doppelgänger, ... *8*

She Had Some Artichokes *9*

Oh Mollusk *10*

Their salt *15*

Dear Oma, ... *16*

Seamstresses of Wind *18*

Swinger *19*

In a previous life *20*

Praise Flowers *21*

This is a love poem *22*

Last Resort *24*

Oh Lady of the Lake *25*

Oh Lady of the Night *26*

The Fire Woman *28*

against closure *29*

Overwhelm *30*

Acknowledgments *36*

Last Resort

I don't know

how the mud flats
or how the prairie grasses
how the garlic scapes or the beet
greens above the soil. I don't know how the blue
berries or how the wind picks up and carries on in a maelstrom
how the night mares or the morning dews.
I don't know how the river knows its way back to the sea
but I do know gravity. The weight and heft of the thing
of living that is. How tenderly you can fall into grass
and hope, despite all signs otherwise, that the world will turn
though I don't know how the world turns only
$$\text{that it does}$$

Earthopomorphizing

Prairie dogs kiss
        but I am anthropomorphizing
according to the googled site
        on prairie dog behavior.
They don't kiss, silly, they simply "touch mouths."

        Are they standing or not standing?
Facing, not facing? Are they not eye to eye?
Not kissing, they touch mouths

        simply to recognize one another.
But isn't a kiss simply a metaphor for recognition
of another scouting mouth
as one realizes the body as the mammalian
murmur of our dark earth?

Doubt Probably

I live with an
irritating, steady
companion called Doubt.

Doubt must be quieted
each morning and reminded
again in the afternoon
to take a rest.

Doubt can be ignored
but doesn't go away
won't move out
or pay the rent.

Doubt Probably
eats my chocolate
when I'm busy working
and then joins me
on the couch each evening

At the River Deschutes:

Asphalt, concrete,
chain-link fence,
lightbulbs, live wires,
New Balance shoes,
paper cups, plastic straws,
and cigarette butts.

How is it we co evolved here,
with the shifting earth
the curving rivers,
the tumbling stones,
the gorge worn by ice and water,
the ferns, mosses, and the weed
gone to seed, the rat in the grass,

and that snake that slides onto a hot rock
and back into the cold river
again?

Oh Tahoma

Salish refers to the Lushootseed language
The Inland Sea received the name.

On this inland sea, there are worlds where words
       slide like water on our tongues
              a world where orcas and otters swim along
in water fed by the Nisqually, the Deschutes, and the Duwamish.
Before us,
before photographs, before bridges or oil trains,
before gardeners or shovels or housing solutions,
Before us,
a misty, mythic world.
And, when we're gone, there will be new worlds,
other estuaries to restore. Nisqually, our example,
reaches a briny tongue, reclaiming tidelands once damned.
Listening to the far Elwha, one hears
salmon travel a river's route home to die.
River revered. River as healer. River as last rite.
Many friends have died here where Salish fingers
reach our shores, where Tahoma's mammoth
rock-heart watches over our watery world,
slumbering in uncertain solidity. Oh Tacoma.
              Tac hom a. The word
                      ends in air, in fire, in awe

A Heron waits

amidst rain, tides, and sky,
    and sidewalks near ferns,
mosses, and evergreen spires,
between politics and communion,
near a bridge where a river is
stopped from meeting the sea, she waits.
Her dragon-metal-grey wings
close with muscular subtlety.
Shoreline shape-shifter, Great Heron
still in silt, in mud, stalks and dives
at this thin, inlet end, competing with seals
where salmon return. Praying by waiting.
Greying the waters toxic,
The 1974 Clean Water Act
permitted pollutants,
flame retardants, polycyclic
aromatic hyrdocarbons -
    mercury, lead, and dioxin.
The grey heron, at the Sound's far finger
beats her wings in three majestic gestures
alights and lands on the near shore. Her dinosaur
wings, a winter-feathered hope.

The world may end in a whimper
but begin again in an estuary

Non-native

They're non-native remarks the milky-eyed lawyer
whose name I don't know but who's joined our table at the pizzeria
on Capitol Way. He's telling his story of a criminal convicted
for swerving and killing   a Possum.

Marsupials (the word swirls round in my mouth). Protectors, these
Possums (they carry their babies in pouches) (an unuttered thought).

Non-native, he continues, *like the grey squirrels*
who weren't here when he was a kid. Disgusting creatures.
(He stays unaware of my musings)   *Ridiculous, he was*
convicted. They're not even native.   He closes his case.

So, I mention the Nutria because I know a bit about nonnative
too, but he's moved on, (so I don't say what I know). Green English
Ivy, Golden Scotch Broom, and Himalayan Blackberry, smothering
the prairies and choking the woodlands, climbing the trunks
of The Western Red Cedar

and brown-eyed me, and blue-eyed lawyer, and plain house sparrow
we're all non-native too. I've gone somewhere beyond
the pizzeria, silently rowing names along our shores
Priest Point Park, Olympia, Mount Rainier,
and the Straits of Juan de Fuca.

Restless waters on my tongue ~
my mouth (a pocket too full to speak)
trying to savor names not my own
Tahoma, Squiatl, Puyallup, Nisqually, and Squaxin

O Possum[1]
Squirrel, Salmon, Swallow

forgive me

I live here

---
1 The word *possum* was borrowed from the Powhatan language (Virginia Algonquian), which (the language, not the word) became extinct in the 1790's when the speakers of the language, under duress, were forced to speak English. (Wikipedia 2018)

Dear Doppelgänger,

For some reason, on the train to Hue, in Vietnam,
I am sitting a few seats behind you and your lover.
And, now, the young man right in front of me
has pulled the blind, so I can't watch the coastline pass by.

For this reason, I look ahead, watching you two ~
you kiss the side of her neck, and confidently reach
one strong arm around her to pull her close. I watch you
slide your hand naturally to her knee, and feel an ache below
my heart that doesn't understand that you are not actually Him.

You don't notice me watching, staring, really,
don't know that you are playing out a drama
of some random woman's long, long grieving.

The young man sitting next to me reaches into a cellophane bag
of perfectly square, white bread.
He gestures me a lipsticked smile, offers a slice, without words.
I decline with a wave of my hand and a smile. He returns to his phone
scrolling through pictures of himself in dresses.

He could not know how his tender offering
holds my heart, still, or could he?
In the train's steady movement, I hear
—not yet, not yet, not yet, not yet

She Had Some Artichokes

—after Joy Harjo

She had some artichokes protecting her pale heart
she had late-august artichokes with purple crowns
she'd had other artichokes that were all thorns

    she'd had a lot of artichokes

she had some artichokes crawling with ants
she had artichokes who taught her to dance

she had artichokes she planted
artichokes she covered in mulch
she had artichokes she lied to
she'd had some artichokes who died, too

she had some artichokes she slept with
she had artichokes who undressed her
she had an artichoke tattooed on her breast
after an artichoke tore through her chest

    she's had a lot of artichokes
    and some people judged her

she plucked them apart, leaf by tender leaf
and once inside, she savored them.

She once had some artichokes, but they weren't really hers
    she ate their hearts whole and when she's gone, they'll eat hers

Oh Mollusk

Oh tender self
Consider: the Oyster's work

and Mussel's (beings without narratives).
I am not forgetting my father
who died with mottled lungs.

He was more gentle
than I ever knew when
he was still breathing.

I saw it in his handwriting,
a list of his siblings and their
ages when they died.

The youngest, he was the last
to go. His mother, a mother
of 5, had one unseeing eye

like a floating Oyster in a socket.
He died after a season of smoke.
He liked Oyster stew.

Oysters from a jar heated in milk.
I found it repulsive.
Grey membranes of whole beings

floating in warm milk.
It took teeth to taste their zinc.
Still he was more gentle than

I ever estimated. It was in
his handwriting, in a note
to my older brother's first

grade teacher, describing him as
eager, social, and curious, not hyper
excessive, or challenging

as we all knew him to be. It took my breath
away: The note. So tender. The unknowable:
essential as the membrane of the grey Oyster

body, holding ourselves together;
holding others apart. The work?
a humble grinding of grit—

Oysters

I wanted to write about them—

    their luminescent pearl essences

            their briny, watery world,
            their cold, slick sexiness

            But I got stuck
            on intelligence

        so I searched the internet for the mind
            of the mollusk

        and found much on the mind
        of the octopus (also a mollusk)
              —but not an oyster—

Did you know some vegans eat them?
    the case could be made
      they're not even
          as sentient as trees

  I have eaten
        an oyster or two raw
whole—

      Their taste: Metallic: zinc-shiny

           shell
      —a map of their world—

        interior—they are, oysters,
    their shells are their stars
        their meteors, their sky—

s   h   u   c   k   e   d

        they reveal
—the whole ocean on a half shell—

A heat wave will kill them. Cook them on the beach.

    Dirty work, they do, pearling—
        filtering what harms us all
            all

murky
      mind   all
            murky heart
      no central nervous system

        Intestinal
        Intelligence: Shell

They do what oysters do. We don't
        know.

    I wanted to draw it
the sharp curve of the shell's edge
      a kind of protection

I wanted
    to merge tidally

                              breath and ocean cold
                 breath and salt
                              or being
                  and not even

b   r   e   a   t   h   i   n   g

          their tender bodies at rest

     Mussels, Clams, Oysters, Snails, Barnacles, Crabs, Sea Stars:

               The die off is stagger
                                   ing

               Oyster   a world
                  I heard

          The world is mine
                              Oyster:

     I have taken you whole, I have eaten, and stagger
                                                   ing

               —I   don't   know—

                                        if you
                         or we
                                 will

          s   u   r   v   i   v   e

Their salt

A chipped bowl
stained table linens
a tattered handkerchief

a pocket-sized aluminum trinket
of the virgin Mary
blessed by the water of Lourdes.

My grandmothers as mothers
held these things, their hands
work passed on to me.

I didn't know them. We had no place,
nor language to share. Can you grieve
what you never knew?

They were from other states, other
continents, each from 500 generations
of farmers.

I keep these things against despair,
use them against the endless new
and new and new that marks our time.

I cherish the wear of years
of decades
a century.

They cooked
and served what they had.
There must have been so much steam.

Soups, stews, potatoes, always
salt. Their salt
in my marrow. Their linens
now in tatters on my table

Dear Oma,

What unlikely winds scattered your eggs from a farm in the Netherlands into *this* future?
Across the Atlantic?

I remember my mom telling me that you believed, one day, at the end of the world, California would slide into the Pacific Ocean. You feared for your daughter, my mother, her future. My mother, not superstitious, seemed not afraid of this, but the prophecy has never left me.

Where did you gather it?
This prophecy of wreckage or reckoning?

I found a record of your marriage in online archives, and your husband's occupation: *Landbauer*. I was startled to read the word, easy enough to translate, Land builder, but not the word I'd known for farmer: *Boer*. Land building: Not a world I'll ever know.

Boer is harsh in the mouth. *Landbauer*, though soothes, like handholder. Hands to build land. What was it like then, to be a landbauer? Did you feel it was yours, or did you belong to him, or the land, the farm? Where was your horizon?

Did you know you were in a threshold between farming and the future? I am trying to build a relationship *here* with *this* land, and with the past

I occupy	trying to	back stitch
to something lost	a lineage	
but not	a line	it is not linear
		inheritance.

I'm trying to reach You
by writing into a future.
Oh, the lonely ache of it

Seamstresses of Wind

The length of water
      over which wind has blown

unobstructed is fetch.
Wind over Harbor Seals

who glide and dive out of sight.
Wind within which Cormorants squawk

and Herons fly / seamstresses of wind.
Their wings stitch time with sight.

Time, in which I am caught,
      the invisible distance one might traverse

                  to fetch a beloved

Swinger

I've lost too many lovers to count
and my daughter doesn't know the half of them
though she will often count and recount over dinner.
The past swings into the present with velocity.

My daughter swings into forgiveness and back out
just as I do over my mother's sins. The original sin?
hanging on too long -

but now how she swings alone, my mother, a swinger
in an old-folks home. She knits and draws and tends
to patio flowers, plays bingo and brain games
that keep her mind sharp. She exclaims when I visit:

I'm my own Boss now, as she swings
her old self into the future
                                    where she never swings alone

In a previous life

Years ago, I consulted a fortune teller
perhaps a tarot or palm reader. The details
I don't recall, but when she said: *In a previous life
you were a nun or a monk.* I felt at once it were true.

I was barely 20—and everything pointed to the future
except this: In a previous life I was a nun or a monk.
This would explain the central tension of my life:

To kneel alone in quiet prayer
              or to splay my body in play, in communion,
with wild abandon?

To bend my body in sacrifice, with a spine curved by the work
of grading papers, or to shed my clothes and plunge into cold, fresh water
and later to slip between cool sheets with the warm body of a lover.

In my next life, I will be a seal, slick and frolicking
in sea water with layers of fat and glistening, oily skin,
gorging on salmon where the river meets the sea. An estuarian being.

I have paid my penance, the Catholic version
of karma, worn the hair-shirt, slept with bedbugs,
and gone without sex for years. In my next life

              I will be released into the sea
            sexy, fat, and free

Praise Flowers

Praise Peonies pink silky petals, inhalation of scent beyond sweet scent; Praise Ranunculus' curling yellow heads bowing in April hail showers, let one or two petals drop down, down, down to Earth; Praise Daphne's subtle leaf lines directing nose to clusters of honey delight ... all early eagerness. Praise the pink Moon and the Possum.

Praise the Daffodil waving yellow, and the Tulips unwavering, tall and erect. Poised. Food for urban deer and hungry peasants during wars. Blue. Praise Blue Hyacinth. Praise Blue.

Praise the lipstick sexiness of the Flowering Red Currant. The brief beauty of Camellia. Praise the White Clematis, the Black Iris and the Clitoris.

Praise all the Bleeding Hearts, praise them, and the creeping Violets and the tiny purple Rosemary flowers, praise them all. All urge: Taste me, pungent or sweet.

Praise the Prairie Dogs and the Pansy faces urging us to be trivial. Praise the flowers, their medicines, their meditations, their sense and sexiness—Praise, praise semen, the sneeze and
                                      our brief little lives

This is a love poem

for a grandchild I long for
and also
                for Tahlequah or J35.

I love you irrationally
as murmur of a future
as mammalian fur
                as mother after mother
after mother

as memory of sweet nursing
at breast, milk colostrum cream
memory is also chemical

                Oxytocin is also love

I love you mysteriously
as ocean depths, sonorous and dark
in corners of dreams, our
                futures

I love as bivalve, with fins, and with all four
chambers of a clambering heart

I wish for you Ocean Moon glow
and long silver sunrises
second chances and
                salt

Figs and Persimmons ripening
soft on winter windowsills
springtimes and

                            oceans
de-polluted, new

I wish for magical Mycelium remediation
of toxins,
                                      pure clean

mother's milk free
of poly-chlorinated bipheynals
or poly-fluoroalkyl substances

I wish for you moments with other
               love—mammals, sweet nuzzle of being to being,
                                              futures

and a love that will carry you for days and miles
over the ocean, not in grief, but in joy
                                  after joy after joy.

Last Resort

There's water on the South polar solar terrain
of Mars. Good news, apparently, for those who see their fate
in abandoning our world of water and lava.

Given a choice, I'll stay behind with other crawling
creatures, living among the rubble. It's a loss I dare not romanticize,
the extinction or escape of the meanest predators.

Walls of fire, rivers of rain, winds of destruction. The suffering.
It seems the lowly though are surest to survive—the scavengers and
foragers, parasites and Fireweed, Clover, Bed Bugs, Sugar Ants
and Ferns, Deer, Raccoon, Rats, Possums, gleaners, and fixers.

So let them go, the shadow kings with their shiny things
and dry-cleaned suits; Let them leave our blue origins,
the ancient paths of ferns, their mother's arms.

Let flow the deep rivers of water and lava
from a jeweled underground of ancient saints,
seeds and larvae, rhizomes, embryos,
mycelium, mitochondrial repair.

Underworld intelligence:
Let it renew
renew while my skin withers
to husk and to dust

Oh Lady of the Lake

Forgive us the absurdities
of jet ski and AC. Relieve us
of our sweltering madness.
Give us stillness. Give us lilies.

Give us dredge. Let us drown
 in your algae bloom. Relieve us
of the hellish heat that domes
our lives with smoky haze. Let us sink

to the depths of your memory: Maternal
waters unfossilize what we have forgotten.

 Let us not forsake potential
your amniotic fluids, frogs
                              a future

Oh Lady of the Night

I sleep at the shrine of Pasiphae, night after night,
after falling asleep watching Netflix. No balm.

I sleep without trying to sleep, but receive
no prophecy. The only image: a knife
in the street. We wait for Astraes's return. The world

she left behind: Bees, balm, bullets, butterflies,
knives, honey, money, hours, California
poppies, asters, star jasmine, sea star, blue
mussels, moon snails, and quail. The heron's crest.

The dream I was after was *the thing itself
and not the myth.* The knife was a light
or a shard of glass in the street. The only word:
reconcile. For all I know, my grandmother prayed

every night. *Ave Maria.* Astraes's ascension
is Mary's assumption, the world left behind.
So much grief. In the morning, I think of her dream
of the second coming. An old woman. A miracle. A fox.

Dawn, the vanishing night sky. The world has too much light.
When I was just 17 and between abortions, I traveled
the inside passage to Alaska. I saw The Northern Lights
Aurora Borealis and mistook them, not for morning,

but for a city, tall towers of blue and white light
in the distance. I was deceived and then corrected.
Not the myth, but the thing itself. An avenue
of a city I once knew was called Aurora, an avenue

of hookers, whores, and women of the night. Pomegranates
and honey for these women. Honey for the world. For the goddesses,
honey. The world I've known has always held too much light.
So light at night, I cannot dream. So light I cannot see

t   h   e   s   t   a   r   s

The Fire Woman

—after Wallace Stevens

One must have a mind of summer
to approach fire and tinder
of fir trees going up in flames;

and have been parched a very long time
to witness spruce crackling with heat,
larches burning dazzle in a distant blaze

of August's red twilight; and not think
of all misery in the speed of inferno
in the sounds of blistering winds

which is the sound of the sun
full of the same mystery
that is burning into the same emptiness

for the dreamer who tends the flames,
and everything else herself, beholds everything
that is not there and nothing that is.

against closure

… Lynn Hejinian quotes Helene Cixous:

> *"A feminine textual body is recognized by the fact that it is always endless, without ending…There's no closure; it doesn't stop."*

…

My daughter tells me
no one wants
to hear other peoples' dreams
unless, she says, you happen to be in them …

…. who wants poetry?

Overwhelm

1. o·ver·whelm /ˌōvər'(h)welm/
verb
definition:

to cover
with water
to submerge

2. Resolution:

Whereas development for duration;

Whereas the City and the Development Group;

*Around the world very few civic bodies can hope
to prevail against construction lobbies (AG);*

Whereas the Development Group intends approximately 478 market-rate rental housing units, retail, restaurant, and recreation, which will provide a benefit;

*No requirement for affordable/ strictly supply and demand /
wealthier people / housing stock.
Affordability is not a requirement (OP);*

Whereas the City's State Environmental Policy Act Responsible Official issued a (DNS) Determination of Non-significance.

*The DNS did not consider the possible environmental impact
of the development itself;*

Whereas a local organization appealed, claiming the City should have considered possible environmental impacts itself, rather than just possible impacts of the Agreement;

The reality is that growth in many coastal cities around the world
now depends on ensuring that a blind eye is turned (AG);

Whereas the Hearing Examiner denied appeal, concluding DNS reflected proper consideration of possible impacts of an agreement and not the impacts of development itself;

Global Warming is a collective predicament and the idea
of a collective has been exiled (AG);

Whereas the council held a public hearing / testimony from the public

Whereas best interest: Development Group;

Climate Change. Big growth will not pay. You will be long gone.
We will pay . We will be left. (MMS)

Now. Therefore, The City approves

3. Development:

Market-Rate Shoreline Development
                      Luxury Development
      Development Development
             Market-Rate Development
                    Luxury Development

                        Development
                Shoreline
Development
        Development
                Luxury Development
                        Shoreline Development
        Luxury Shoreline Development
                        Development
                Development
                        Market-Rate Development
    Development Development Development Development
Development Development Development Development   De-
velopment   Development Development   Development
Development   Development   Development Develop-
ment Development Development   Development   Develop-
ment Development   Development   Development Develop-
ment Development   Development   Development
Development Development Development Development Development Development Development Development Development Development Development Development Development Development
Development Development   Development   Development
Development Development Development Development Development Development Development Development Development Development Development Development Development
Development Development   Development   Development
Development Development Development Development Development Development Development Development Development   De-
velopment Development Development Development Development
Development Development Development Development
Development Development Development Development Development

4. Surroundings:

Water birds fly near the shore.

    Water birds fly away.

        Fly away when a human shows up.

Herons
    gulls
        cormorants
            kingfishers
  eagles....soar   shoreline bluffs

barnacles   urban shoreline   Salish Sea

    mud shrimp   neighborhood shoreline ravines

      upland properties   brownfield

    Budd Inlet   logging trucks

      low-dissolved oxygen

Coho Salmon   Deschutes River Estuary resident

    Orcas   Barrow's Golden-eye

    Schneider Creek   dioxides

      furans

                              phthalates

              blight   contaminated land   eye sore

                        red-breasted Merganser   resident Orcas

              Oyster reef   desolate-

waterfront   humans   common Merganser

                Cut-throat Trout   sea-level rise

Loons   tidal currents   intertidal wetlands

              oil-barge unloading   eye-sore

neighborhood   ecosystem preservation   Garfield Creek

              benthic dioxin   nutrient overload   tank farms

home less   eye sore
              endangered salmon   contaminated land   sand
                    rookery   endangered orca
erosion   blight   homeless   estuary   shore
        crabs   mussels   clams   perch
          flounder   tideland   Ruddy Duck
                cobbles and gravel
                  mudflat   logging trucks
            steep-slope topography
future generations   Hooded Merganser
          humans   Ghost Shrimp   Gulls   Grebes

Blue Heron

    fly away when a human shows up …

Acknowledgments

"I don't know" was first published in *Works in Progress*, a local independent newspaper of Olympia, Washington.

"A Heron .. is waiting" was published as an earlier version in a video series of PNW poets: *Unspoken Northwest*.

The poems "Non-native" and "Last Resort" were published as earlier versions in *Subjectiv :Visual and Literary Arts of the Pacific Northwest*.

In the poem, "Non-native," which I wrote in 2018, I include the name Priest Point Park. The park is now named Squaxin Park after The Olympia City Council unanimously voted to honor the Squaxin Tribe in 2022.

"She Had Some Artichokes" was inspired by Joy Harjo's "She Had Some Horses"

Italicized phrases in "Oysters!" come from Glenn Garner's article "Millions of Shellfish Boiled Alive Due to Pacific Northwest Heatwave," and from Bob Granleese's article "Are Oysters Vegan?" The Guardian online, September 2019.

In "Oh Lady of the Night," the lines "the thing itself / and not the myth" are from Adrienne Rich's poem "Diving into the Wreck;" inspiration for this poem also comes from Lucille Clifton's poem "My dream about the second coming."

The poem "The Fire Woman" was inspired by and modeled after Wallace Stevens's poem "The Snow Man."

Texts borrowed from for the found poem "OverWhelm" include:

• Resolution No M-2206 by Olympia City Council passed on March 30th 2021, which approved, with one council-member opposing, a legally-binding contract on a 15-year development agreement for market-rate housing with no requirement for an Environmental Impact Statement based on a city official's determination of non-significance (DNS).

• Olympia Ecosystems Preservation's explanation of their appeal of the city's decision.
• Comments from Olympia citizens and organizations regarding the 15 year West Bay Yards Development Agreement.
• (AG) Amitav Gosh's book: The Great Derangement: Climate Change and the Unthinkable.
• (OP) An email from an Olympia City Planner in response to a citizen concern about affordable housing.
• (MMS) Students from Marshall Middle School, Citizen Science Initiative, letter to Olympia City Council.

Thank you to family and friends who have encouraged my poetry writing and my quirky ways of seeing the world, with special thanks to Thea and Joren for their support, to Jennifer Berney for her careful reading of the poems that make up this collection and many more that were set aside, to Jane Wong and Stefania Heim for their guidance into the vast world of poetry and ongoing support, to Cecily Schmidt for artistic collaborations, and to Val Markus and Allison Imel for timeless friendships and enduring love. Thank you, dear ones.

Special thanks to Robert Ross and Last Word Press for bringing these poems into the world, for excellent editorial advice, and fun conversations about book making. I can't imagine a better home for these poems.

Kathleen Byrd holds an MFA from Western Washington University. She lives in Olympia, Washington, where she teaches English and creative writing. Her work has previously appeared in *Subjectiv: visual and literary arts of the Pacific Northwest, Pontoon, Crosscurrents, Works in Progress, The Bear Deluxe Magazine*, among others.